Best Wishes
Sean
J---

GW00507766

Quickening
of the Sand

Anthology of Poems by Shane Moore O'Sullivan

Quickening of the Sand

Published by IPC Ltd
Unit 4, Woodbury Business Park, Woodbury, Exeter,
Devon, EX5 1AY

Editor: Matthew Boyden

First edition: March 2016

Printed & bound in the UK

All proceeds from the sale of this book (net of all production costs)
shall be allocated to St Petrock's, Exeter's charity for people who are
homeless or vulnerably housed.

For Julia

CONTENTS   PAGE NO.

INTRODUCTION

SHANE MOORE O'SULLIVAN

Like many other English writers with first generation Irish roots, Shane O'Sullivan has been influenced strongly by expatriate disorientation, whilst never having actually lived in Ireland. This geographical distance caused him to immerse himself in the Irish literary canon, with inevitable emphasis on the works of Wilde, Yeats, Joyce, Flan O'Brian and Heaney. Absinthe, during six years living in Southern France, did not make Shane's heart any fonder (other than for his fellow Irish-French émigré Samuel Beckett), and it was only after returning full-time to England, and life in Devon, that he was able to place himself creatively within his environment. O'Sullivan has become a Devonian poet, a narrow and reluctant locus of reference that has, despite the breadth of his influences, enabled him to create finally a volume of poetry that he is happy to publish. It follows that, while this collection is rooted in the land and the people around O'Sullivan's home in Exeter, his language is Irish in its self-conscious and shameless lyricism. The collection's highly personal narratives, all of which are coloured profoundly by experience, feed the truism that all poets think in the first person – to which end this collection testifies as much to its author's defining concerns for meaning and identity, as to his abiding search for expression.

Matthew Boyden, February 2016

RICHARD THORN

Richard Thorn is a member of the Royal Institute of Painters in Water Colours. He lives and works in the Teign Valley in Devon.

Both his original line drawings and water colours have been especially commissioned for this publication.

MATINS, CHRISTMAS MORNING, EXETER CATHEDRAL

Candles burn bright,
the stone of the chapel wall flickers yellow gold;
Shadows dance,
projected like ghosts onto this theatre of light;
Lone chorister's voice pierces the air,
its resonance fills the void,
As peeling bells welcome worshippers
in from the dark and out of cold.

Scent of starched linen,
candlewax and incense,
and shoe polish,
and perfume and soap;
Smiles and secret greetings,
between those that are to each other already known;
Procession of the choir with acolytes to the rear,
ushered into their allotted seats;
The organ warms,
the conductor gives the cue;
the perennial ritual begins.

FORGIVENESS

Gwydion, bring my horse home from this world,
of Shamans and Hermits;
Ride the trusting animal,
with your heels and hands of silk.
He will carry you safely
along the paths of the darkening wood.

Keep away from Medb and her drunken screams;
And if you hear their echo in the forest glade,
Do not become ensnared by her charms,
as she peddles only in betrayal and soiled dreams.

Child of Don,
do nor spur my horse,
nor harness his mouth with steel;
And when you both safely return,
pass his halter rope to me,
So that I might hold him for the very last time,
before we set him free.

BUDLEIGH SALTERTON

S tabbing shock from the icy sea,
like needles under the skin;
As I dive into Budleigh Bay,
its waters as clear as gin.
Swirling foam,
pouring down my ears,
and the sting of salt in my eye;
And on my back I float,
looking up at a cloudless sky.

Soft sandstone of the cliff face,
sculptured in Ceylonese red;
And windows carved in the rock,
like an advent calendar on this ancient pebble bed;
While terns spin and dip on a thermal,
as sandpipers skim the beach;
Gentle waves push my sandals up onto the stone,
and just out of reach.

Fisherman's wide back,
boot leather tanned,
bends over to grease the pulley chain;
His face and arms as if from some distant land,
Hemingway's keys or Millais' tales of ancient Spain.
He repairs the net with a timeless hand,
and fills the waiting boat with hook, rod and buoy;
A sea hunter alone with the day,
defiant upon the pebble beach of Budleigh Bay.

QUICKENING OF THE SAND

Would you banish me to far-off St Helena?
Would you abandon me to some strange and foreign land?
Even though you own the silver in my heart,
Until the quickening of the sand.

You will not kiss me in the Kashmir Garden,
Nor amongst its rocks hold me,
in a lovers' embrace;
And you will never feel the feather buds of the magnolia,
With your hands entwined with mine,
and with love etched upon your face.

We shall never share the pink flowers of the primula,
brought from India in 1842;
And I shall never walk beside you,
and carry your books on my back,
the way we did at school.
You will never enter the secret walled garden,
with its open door flaked with peeling paint,
For the cord was cut some time ago,
so as to safeguard and preserve the status quo.

Do not leave me,
at the Gates of All Souls in Naples,
exiled amongst the dead;
Left to contemplate,
a piteous end with rooks,
circling around my head.
Do not exile me to far off St. Helena;
abandon me to some strange and unfamiliar land;
Even though you own the silver in my heart,
until the quickening of the sand.

OPEN WARFARE

Five machine guns rattle,
and a Howitzer boom;
And thoughts of innocent Wilfred flood in;
Nearly one hundred years of war,
since that winter's day,
He sought to hide his body,
From a thousand fragments of metal,
Behind the stem of a single poppy.*

One hundred years,
of slaughtered innocence;
In a world so beautiful from space;
One hundred years,
of jingoism, nationalism, hatred and pride;
One hundred years,
of greed, vanity, misunderstanding and insanity;
In what should be a home,
and garden of serenity.

Just another name on the village memorial,
and no lesson learnt;
Another innocent victim,
another sacrificial soul;
To save a future generation,
from this endless repetition;
From this cycle of destruction,
that permeates and ferments,
This devilry, this open warfare.

*The stem of a single poppy is attributed to Wilfred Owen's last letter home
from the Front before he was killed in the final week of the Great War 1918.*

DEATH OF A DOCTOR MY FATHER

He sat in his wicker chair,
fingers curled around the heavy crystal glass,
Nicotine coloured whisky,
swirling and falling over large cubes of ice;
Lonely,
empty chairs surrounded him,
the club collegiate now all gone;
As death sat on his shoulder,
and whispered that which he already knew;
That when it came to parties;
he was always the first to arrive,
and never left on cue.

He lay in his hospital bed,
defeated,
after a difference of opinion with his physician;
For at eighty-seven,
he thought himself,
too old to die from a disease of the bone,
Too old to die,
from a poisoned heart,
and perhaps too old to die at all;
And as I looked into his eyes,
for the very last time,
I saw in them a look so grim;
For finally he realised that the bell that tolls for all of us,
was about to toll for him.

A TAXI DRIVER FORESEES THE COMING OF A SATURDAY NIGHT

The dogs have gone insane;
owners have spread neurosis down their leads,
and into their veins;
Controllers are abroad with their poisoned seeds,
and gossip from around the guillotine.
The carparks are full,
and the shopping centres gurgle,
with obesity and excess;
Madness ensues,
and in the coming of the dark,
torrents of rain will soon be running with blood.

The soul is on the moor,
and will not address these idols,
with perfunctory greetings anymore;
Mist and solitude are all around,
yet up here no loneliness abounds.
The cottage door is open,
and the grate is full of oak and ash,
ready to be lit;
The dog looks up and spirits lift,
for at the side of my bed,
an open poetry book, half-read.

THE LAKE IN AUTUMN

Fallen leaves of burnt ochre,
amber and gold;
Leaves of blood-red crimson,
and faded apple green,
Lie in a still mosaic,
on the surface of the lake.
And in between the oak,
and stripped bark of the eucalyptus;
Under the smoky filter of a dappled light,
A stream laps the stone,
hisses and passes out of sight.

Pair of bleached poplars sway,
in a gentle courtship;
In front of a pale blue sky.
While a date palm stands solitary,
as if exiled from a warmer place;
And leaves of orange-vermillion from a nearby acer,
in an apron around its base.
Towering dark shadow of a cedar,
planted years ago,
Perhaps by someone who understood,
that whatever comes must also go.

Shock of yellow from the honey locust tree,
and saintly arc of the beach;
Shimmering leaves of the silver birch,
that crest and fall like stardust,
And form tears like those of some delicate chandelier;
Thin line of wood smoke rising,
vertically into a now breathless sky.

And I, sitting on this felled oak,
With roots twisted and tangled,
with dock and bramble;
And rendered with stone,
and light-coloured clay,
Stare dreamlike into the far reaches of the lake.

Is this your reflection on the surface of the water,
or is it my mistake?
Is your love still burning,
or is it all too late?
Would I trade absolution from this pain
of forever being apart;
And exchange it,
for never having shared a moment with you,
In this our only space,
and in this our only time?

Despite attempts to arrest its course,

with defiant gestures designed to leave no trace;

Changing seasons reveal life as nothing more,

than the briefest of interludes;

While the gentle humility of love endures,

forever.

GOODBYE

From under the canopy of the station,
with its backdrop of Portland Stone;

You appear in all your beauty,

and walk to me as if it were always meant;

At this rendezvous for lovers,

this crossroads of helloes and goodbyes,

At this brief encounter,

you pretend that our meeting is nothing more,

than a daily event.

Yet, I had already stared deep into your painted eye,

and felt the stir and delight in your soul,

And you had already held my love,

in the palm of your gentle hand.

Look down from the Bishop's Palace,

through its mullioned windows,

and onto the felted lawn,

Allow your eyes to rest upon the American Walnut tree;

And as you sit at the far end of the vaulted crypt,

cocooned in an enviously simple faith,

Pray for me,

that this eternal haunting may soon come to an end.

THE INNOCENT SPY

Thank you for driving me to the station;
   And thank you for carrying my suitcases to the platform.
My name is Menshikova;
I am Honourable lawyer,
of The Russian Federation.

Jack, you are guilty of a serious crime;
And it would be better for you if you,
came to Moscow as soon as you have time.
Alternatively I shall be obliged to return,
and to find you;
So I prefer for you to comply,
with this my polite request.

There must have been some mistake,
for I am not a spy!
I have only read a biography of Philby,
and a small article about George Blake.
I was never very fond of Blunt,
as I thought his taste in art a little too opaque;
Surely this whole episode is a dream,
or some terrible mistake?

There is no mistake,
except the one you yourself have made;
You were aware at the moment of the crime,
that your actions were wrong;
As you knew where this caprice might lead all along;
Your only mitigation will be,
if you come to Moscow now with me.

I have never been to Russia,
and have only seen Dr Zhivago once,
and Anna Karenina twice;
I did enjoy the daffodils and the snow,
and in the latter loved Garbo,
in her black and white.
Please tell me Honourable lawyer,
what I have done,
To offend the great Federation of Russia,
in all its might.

You are guilty,
of the worst crime known to a man;
you have broken a loved one's heart;
And like the fallen Icarus,
or the humbled Wilde,
you have sailed too close to the sun.

BELVEDERE TOWER

Banks of grey and yellow,
fragments of cloud,
remnants from some far off Atlantic storm
Roll over the flooded estuary,
in ribbons fast and true;
And underneath, another charcoaled layer,
with smudged edges and vapour fingers,
That curl and swirl,
and sometimes disappear.

Tiny jewels of flickering light,
from the street lamps of the harbour;
And on the horizon a thin line of sea,
fused with blinding silver and a hint of lapis blue;
Across to my right and high up amongst the trees,
a solitary tower overlooks the scene;
And falling away a line of saturated fields,
dressed in an English winter green.

Climbing up to the tower,
and resting in its garden,
flecked with rhododendron;
And finding an open space,
in the canopy of its trees,
Look down upon the flooded estuary,
to Topsham, Lympstone, Exmouth and the sea;
And far off in the northern distance,
count all the dark hills that lie between you and me.

ETERNITY

If I am to die in exile,
let me not be soaked in absinthe;
If I am to die in pain,
let me not cry out in agony;
If I am to die in public please,
let it be with dignity;
If I am to die shunned by friends,
let me not be angry;
If I am to die without you, then,
let my death be solitary.

NIGEL

We surveyed the track from the concrete wall,
on the sea side of the Dawlish main line;
As salt spray from winter breakers,
licked our stinging cheeks,
and gusts of wind blew into our hair;
And we laughed,
and imagined this moment lasting longer than forever;
Pulled by icy blasts,
of cold Atlantic air.

He lay across the rail at the crossing
And listened for the sound,
of the oncoming train;
He gave out a shriek of delight,
as he made his escape,
just before it came;
And after it had passed,
he lay down again,
in the teeth of the swirling rain;
"My kingdom for a horse," he said.
"My kingdom for a horse";
and looked up at me so desperately.

In Powderham church garden,

just above the mainline,

I sit and weep.

As I remember him and reflect upon the awful deed;

And how on one dark and lonely winter's night,

wild-eyed and terrified,

He ended it all,

by standing in front of the London train.

My dearest friend,

I have a horse for you,

but am afraid it is all too late.

CASTLE DROGO & KILLERTON HOUSE

Scream of the chainsaw,
splits the air.
The executioners arrive,
yellow fluorescent jackets,
and red mufflers on their heads,
And in the time it has taken to write these lines,
two hundred years of growth are dead.

Directors from the Trust,
decide to erect another fence,
made from the same fallen tree;
And on this fence,
another sign to show us what they think,
we all should see.
Members of the Trust,
please erect another mural,
and place it high up in the canopy,
So that you may replace the natural view,
God's timeless gift to us,
with man-made photography.

Stale scones and formica from the café,
in the courtyard of this once stately home;
No Lady Ottoline to welcome us all,
for homemade tea on the chequered lawn;
No gilded leather books of poetry,
in fine vellum, marigold and Aegean blue;
No fire in the hearth,
no wild swans at Coole,
and long gone Lady Gregory.
And within these Ravenna's walls,
neither love nor jovial company;
Just a shop and a till,
selling jam and drab imported souvenirs.

ANGEL

You sent me an angel yesterday;
        And then, in your wisdom, you took her away.
I am not angry.
I am just sad;
Because she left a tear
On the stained-glass window,
that looks out from my broken heart.

WILD FLOWERS

In my mind your colour is straw yellow;
        And while out walking the wood,
I spot a single charlock;
And peering over a Devon hedge,
A carpet of meadow buttercups appear.

This morning on the Long Walk,
Adorned in warm spring sunlight,
There are tiny yellow primroses everywhere.

In my mind your colour is sea holly powder blue.
The rose pink of the musk mallow is also you;
Chalk white petals of the daisy and wild angelica too;
Pale pastel mauve and a sprinkle of violet from the field pansy
And a single red poppy is on my palette too;
It is in the colours of wild flowers,
that I shall always remember you.